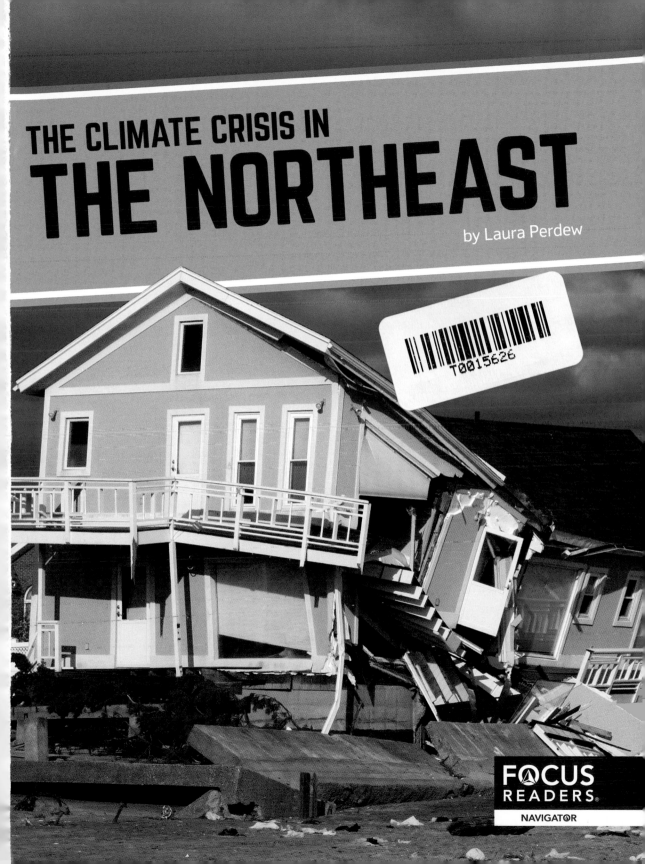

THE CLIMATE CRISIS IN
THE NORTHEAST

by Laura Perdew

T0015626

FOCUS READERS

NAVIGATOR

WWW.FOCUSREADERS.COM

Focus Readers is distributed by North Star Editions:
sales@northstareditions.com | 888-417-0195

Produced for Focus Readers by Red Line Editorial.

Content Consultant: Trevor J. Krabbenhoft, PhD, Assistant Professor of Biological Sciences, University at Buffalo

Photographs ©: Shutterstock Images, cover, 1, 8–9, 14–15, 17, 22–23; Matt Rourke/AP Images, 4–5; Edward Lea/The Press of Atlantic City/AP Images, 6; Red Line Editorial, 10; John Normile/Getty Images News/Getty Images, 12; iStockphoto, 19; Efren Landaos/Sipa USA/AP Images, 21; Charles Krupa/AP Images, 24; Wilson Ring/AP Images, 27; Dave Zajac/Record-Journal/AP Images, 28

Library of Congress Cataloging-in-Publication Data
Names: Perdew, Laura, author.
Title: The climate crisis in the Northeast / by Laura Perdew.
Description: Lake Elmo, MN : Focus Readers, [2024] | Series: The climate
    crisis in America | Includes index. | Audience: Grades 4-6
Identifiers: LCCN 2023002938 (print) | LCCN 2023002939 (ebook) | ISBN
    9781637396308 (hardcover) | ISBN 9781637396872 (paperback) | ISBN
    9781637397954 (ebook) | ISBN 9781637397442 (pdf)
Subjects: LCSH: Endangered ecosystems--Northeastern States--Juvenile
    literature. | Biodiversity--Climatic factors--Northeastern
    States--Juvenile literature.
Classification: LCC QH76.5.N96 H88 2024 (print) | LCC QH76.5.N96 (ebook)
    | DDC 577.27--dc23/eng/20230124
LC record available at https://lccn.loc.gov/2023002938
LC ebook record available at https://lccn.loc.gov/2023002939

Printed in the United States of America
Mankato, MN
082023

ABOUT THE AUTHOR

Laura Perdew is a mom, writing consultant, and author of more than 50 books for children. She writes both fiction and nonfiction with a focus on nature, the environment, and environmental issues. She lives and plays in Boulder, Colorado.

TABLE OF CONTENTS

CHAPTER 1

IDA HITS THE NORTHEAST

In September 2021, Tropical Storm Ida reached the Northeast region. By then, it was no longer a hurricane. But it was still a monster storm. It dumped record rainfall on the region in a short amount of time. It caused several tornadoes. There was flash flooding in cities. All of these events happened quickly.

Flooding from Tropical Storm Ida damaged cars in many northeastern cities, including Philadelphia, Pennsylvania.

A house in New Jersey was destroyed after one of Ida's tornadoes swept through the area.

In New York City, many streets were like canals. Floodwater swept away people in cars. Subway tunnels flooded, and trains sat underwater. Parks looked like swimming pools. Water poured into homes through windows and doors. Stranded people waited hours for rescue. Dozens of people died.

Ida was an extreme storm fueled by **climate change**. This crisis is raising average temperatures all over the world. Warmer air can hold more moisture. This allows storms to grow bigger and stronger more quickly.

WEATHER OR CLIMATE?

An area might have one day that is hot and humid. Another day might be cool and rainy. These conditions are the area's weather. Weather describes a short period of time in one place. It includes temperature, humidity, **precipitation**, and more. An area's climate involves the same conditions. But climate is the pattern of those weather conditions over a long period of time.

CHAPTER 2

CLIMATE OF THE NORTHEAST

The Northeast has four separate seasons. These seasons bring a wide variety of temperatures and weather. Temperatures also vary from north to south. Maine, New Hampshire, and Vermont are farther north. These states have milder summers. New Jersey, Delaware, and Maryland are farther

The fall makes forests across the Northeast colorful. It draws visitors to places such as New Hampshire's Franconia Notch State Park.

south. Their summers tend to be warm and humid.

Other features also play a role. For example, the Appalachian Mountains run through most Northeast states. Temperatures are cooler higher up.

THE NORTHEAST

The Atlantic Ocean impacts the coast. Most Northeast states, including Massachusetts, Rhode Island, and Connecticut, have coastlines. In coastal areas, the ocean keeps temperatures more consistent. So, coastal areas have warmer winters than inland areas. Also, coastal summers tend to be cooler.

The ocean affects precipitation, too. Air currents collect ocean moisture. That air then moves inland. As a result, the Northeast receives frequent precipitation all year. Winters can be icy and snowy.

Jet streams are also important. Jet streams are winds that blow high up in the atmosphere. They move from west to

In December 2022, a strong lake-effect storm left some homes in Western New York frozen over by ice.

east. They often pass over the Northeast. Jet streams can carry storms with them.

The Great Lakes affect weather, too. Lake Erie borders northwestern Pennsylvania and part of New York. Lake Ontario borders New York as well. In the fall and winter, cold air blows over the warmer lake water. Snowstorms often form. This is known as lake-effect snow.

The region's climate supports vast forests. People have depended on these forests for thousands of years. Many **Indigenous** groups developed forest gardens. The gardens grew berries, nuts, and more. They sustained people and attracted animals. As a result, people more easily hunted elk, deer, and bear.

NOR'EASTERS

Nor'easters are storms with spiraling winds. They got their name because the strong winds blow over the region from the northeast. They form along the Atlantic coast. Cold air from the jet stream meets the warmer water of the Atlantic. These are the perfect ingredients for a big storm.

CHAPTER 3

A CLIMATE EMERGENCY

Climate change is raising Earth's average temperatures. The Northeast is warming faster than most other US regions. Between 1900 and 2020, some areas got more than 3.5 degrees Fahrenheit (1.9°C) hotter. Higher temperatures mean heat waves are more

Northeast cities, such as Providence, Rhode Island, are especially impacted by climate change. They face extra risks of heat and flooding.

common. Heat waves are also more intense and long-lasting.

In addition, parts of the Northeast are densely populated. Millions of people live in cities. These urban areas create heat islands. Roads, buildings, and other human-made structures absorb heat. They do not cool as easily as natural areas. As a result, hot days are even hotter in urban areas.

Higher temperatures are also impacting coastal areas. Glaciers are melting. As a result, ocean water levels are rising. This rise is leading to more intense flooding along the Atlantic coast. **Storm surges** are more dangerous, too.

The entire state of Delaware is a coastal area. Floods from rising tides and storm surges are a major threat.

The region is also facing more rain and snow. The number of extreme precipitation events is increasing, too. These events involve heavy rains over a short period of time. Scientists expect that trend to continue. It is likely to lead to more frequent flooding.

Other areas of the Northeast face seasonal droughts. One cause of these droughts is earlier snowmelt. Another cause is faster snowmelt. Plus, higher temperatures mean greater evaporation. And when downpours occur, water does not soak into the ground. Instead, it

GREENHOUSE GASES

Humans burn huge amounts of **fossil fuels**. Burning them produces **greenhouse gas emissions**. Some gases enter the atmosphere. There, they trap heat. That causes climate change. Oceans also absorb greenhouse gases. This increases **ocean acidity**. A more acidic ocean causes many changes. Shellfish off the Northeast coast are one example. They need strong shells. But ocean acidity makes building those strong shells harder. Fewer shellfish survive. That harms the region's seafood industries.

The blue crab is a big part of Maryland's economy. It is also a key species in the Chesapeake Bay.

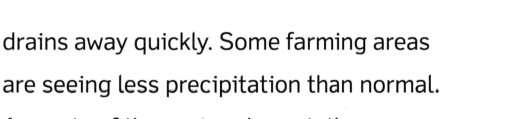

drains away quickly. Some farming areas are seeing less precipitation than normal. As parts of the region dry out, they are more at risk for wildfires.

These changes are happening slowly. But the changes add up over time. They are having major impacts across the Northeast.

KIDS FIGHT CLIMATE CHANGE

Ajani Stella became a climate activist at a young age. At 10 years old, he spoke at a meeting in New York City. The meeting was about teachers' pensions. Pensions are a way of saving for retirement. Ajani argued that the pension funds should stop investing in fossil fuel companies. Investing means putting money toward something to help it succeed. So, Ajani's idea could help cut fossil fuel use.

Ajani didn't stop there. A few years later, he started a new group. It is called Kids Fight Climate Change. Young people lead this group. They focus on a few areas. One is education. The group helps teach climate science in a clear way. Kids Fight Climate Change also helps young people use this

Ajani Stella (second from left) attends an event with other young climate activists in 2022.

knowledge. It shows people how they can take action. From there, young people can become leaders. Their action and leadership can lead to a more sustainable future.

CHAPTER 4

ADAPTING TO CHANGE

The Northeast region aims to reduce greenhouse gas emissions. One plan is to shift to renewable energy. Wind and solar power already provide clean energy to millions of people. More projects are underway.

Transportation is another major contributor to greenhouse gas

In 2021, approximately one-quarter of Maine's electricity came from wind power.

Boston mayor Michelle Wu was one of the first city leaders in the United States to run on climate action.

emissions. Lowering those emissions can help. In 2022, the mayor of Boston, Massachusetts, took action. She made several bus lines free to users. The program aims to provide equal access to transportation. It also addresses climate and air-quality issues. The hope is that more people will use public transportation. Buses can transport people using far less energy per person than cars. As a result, increased bus use can lower emissions.

Even so, climate change is already here. So, people in the Northeast must also adapt. A first step is more research. Scientists gather data to track climate change. This information can show where climate impacts will be the greatest. For instance, one area might face especially intense heat effects. Knowing this information helps leaders plan.

State and local projects are already happening. For example, floods wash pollutants into waterways. They also cause erosion. All of this reduces water quality. In Vermont, workers replaced more than 1,000 culverts. A culvert is a tunnel that guides water under roads. The new culverts meet the needs of a changing climate. They are larger. They protect against flooding. They also make it easier for fish to swim upstream.

Many cities are also using natural areas to protect against flooding. They are protecting wetlands, coastlines, forests, and parks. These areas soak up water.

Other projects create natural methods to collect, filter, and absorb stormwater. For instance, people can use rain barrels. These barrels collect rainwater from

A new culvert (left, background) in Vermont can be seen near an old culvert (right).

gutters. People then use the rainwater for lawns and gardens. Also, a new type of pavement allows water to pass through. The water goes into the ground. These methods reduce the water that ends up in sewers. That means less flooding.

Other projects focus on heat. New York City is working to protect people's health during heat waves. The city is providing

In 2020, Meriden, Connecticut, built new pipes under the ground to help prevent flooding.

more cooling centers. The city is also working to reduce the heat island effect. One solution is using reflective roofs on buildings. These types of roofs absorb less heat.

Individuals can also help. They can spread the word about the crisis. Writing letters or emails to lawmakers can lead to new climate laws. Taking part in protests brings attention to the climate crisis. Students can also work to make their school more climate-friendly. Together, actions both large and small can help in the fight against climate change.

CLIMATE CHANGE AND HEALTH

Heat waves and poor air quality affect physical health. Extreme weather and flooding put people at risk for injury. Mentally, the climate crisis causes increased anxiety. Low-income areas and communities of color are more likely to be affected. In addition, these communities have less access to health care. As a result, investing in health care can help people adapt to climate change.

FOCUS ON
THE NORTHEAST

Write your answers on a separate piece of paper.

1. Write a letter to a local lawmaker explaining three reasons why people should care about climate change.

2. In your opinion, what is the Northeast's greatest threat from climate change?

3. When did Tropical Storm Ida hit the Northeast?

    A. 2020

    B. 2021

    C. 2022

4. Why do cities tend to be hotter than the natural areas around them?

    A. Most cities do not have air conditioners or other ways of cooling down.

    B. On average, cities have more sunny days than natural areas.

    C. Roads and buildings absorb heat rather than reflecting it.

Answer key on page 32.

GLOSSARY

climate change
A human-caused global crisis involving long-term changes in Earth's temperature and weather patterns.

fossil fuels
Energy sources that come from the remains of plants and animals that died long ago.

greenhouse gas emissions
Gases that are released into the atmosphere by factories, cars, and other sources, leading to climate change.

Indigenous
Native to a region, or belonging to ancestors who lived in a region before colonists arrived.

ocean acidity
A human-caused change in the chemical properties of ocean water that causes coral skeletons and animal shells to weaken.

precipitation
Water that falls from clouds to the ground. It can be in the form of rain, hail, or snow.

storm surges
Risings of the sea that are caused by storms' winds.

TO LEARN MORE

BOOKS

Henzel, Cynthia Kennedy. *Redesigning Cities to Fight Climate Change*. Lake Elmo, MN: Focus Readers, 2023.

Huddleston, Emma. *Adapting to Climate Change*. Minneapolis: Abdo Publishing, 2021.

Minoglio, Andrea. *Our World Out of Balance: Understanding Climate Change and What We Can Do*. San Francisco: Blue Dot Kids Press, 2021.

NOTE TO EDUCATORS

Visit **www.focusreaders.com** to find lesson plans, activities, links, and other resources related to this title.

INDEX

Answer Key: 1. Answers will vary; **2.** Answers will vary; **3.** B; **4.** C